Reflections on a Gift of Watermelon Pickle...

AND OTHER MODERN VERSE

Reflections on a Gift of Watermelon Pickle...

AND OTHER MODERN VERSE

compiled by

STEPHEN DUNNING

EDWARD LUEDERS

HUGH SMITH

SCHOLASTIC BOOK SERVICES
NEW YORK · TORONTO · LONDON · AUCKLAND · SYDNEY · TOKYO

For reprint permission grateful acknowledgment is made to:

Sally Andresen for "Fall" by Sally Andresen.

The Antioch Press for "On Watching the Construction of a Skyscraper" by
Burton Raffel from *Antioch Review* (Winter 1960-61), ©1960 by The Antioch
Press.

Atheneum Publishers for "Cheers," "How to Eat a Poem," and "Ounce" from
IT DOESN'T ALWAYS HAVE TO RHYME by Eve Merriam, ©1964 by Eve
Merriam.

The Atlantic Monthly Co. for "Forgive My Guilt" by Robert P. Tristram Coffin,
copyright 1949 by The Atlantic Monthly Co., Boston, Mass.

Brandt & Brandt for "Twin Lakes Hunter" by A. B. Guthrie, ©1964 by Harper's
Magazine, Inc.

Curtis Brown, Ltd. for "Valentine" from EXILES AND MARRIAGES by Donald
Hall, ©1955 by Donald Hall.

The Christian Science Monitor for "Unfolding Bud" by Naoshi Koriyama, ©1957
by The Christian Science Publishing Society.

John Ciardi for "Elegy for Jog" from AS IF by John Ciardi, copyright 1955 by the
Trustees of Rutgers College.

Communications Advisors, Inc. for "Apartment House" by Gerald Raftery from
The New York Sun.

The Curtis Publishing Co. for "November Day" by Eleanor Averitt from *The
Saturday Evening Post*, ©1958 The Curtis Publishing Co.

August Derleth for the following selections from *Hawk & Whippoorwill:* "A
Coney Island Life" by James L. Weil (Autumn 1961); "The Crows" by Leah
Bodine Drake (Autumn 1960); "The Ne'er-Do-Well" by Arthur M. Sampley
(Autumn 1962). ©1961, 1960, 1962 by August Derleth for *Hawk & Whippoorwill.*

Doubleday & Co., Inc. for "The Bat," copyright 1939 by Theodore Roethke from
WORDS FOR THE WIND by Theodore Roethke; "The Builders," ©1961 by Sara
Henderson Hay from THE STORY HOUR by Sara Henderson Hay. Originally
appeared in *Saturday Review;* "Child on Top of a Greenhouse" by Theodore
Roethke, copyright 1946 by Editorial Publications, Inc., from WORDS FOR THE
WIND by Theodore Roethke; "The Child's Morning," ©1963 by Winfield
Townley Scott from CHANGE OF WEATHER by Winfield Townley Scott. Ap-
peared in *Saturday Review;* "Legacy" by Christopher Morley from THE MID-
DLE KINGDOM, copyright 1944 by Harcourt, Brace & World, Inc. Reprinted
in THE BALLAD OF NEW YORK AND OTHER POEMS by Christopher Morley,
published by Doubleday & Co., Inc.

E. P. Dutton & Co., Inc. for "Ancient History" from LYRIC LAUGHTER by Arthur
Guiterman, copyright 1939 by E. P. Dutton & Co., Inc.; "On the Vanity of
Earthly Greatness" from GAILY THE TROUBADOUR by Arthur Guiterman,
copyright 1936 by E. P. Dutton & Co., Inc., renewal ©1964 by Vido Lindo
Guiterman.

Norma Millay Ellis for "Counting-Out Rhyme" by Edna St. Vincent Millay from
COLLECTED POEMS, Harper & Row, copyright 1928, 1955 by Edna St. Vincent

11th printing .... October 1971

Printed in the U.S.A.

4

Millay and Norma Millay Ellis.

Ann Elmo Agency for "Deer Hunt" by Judson Jerome from *Poetry Magazine* (May 1955), ©1955 by Judson Jerome.

EPOS for "Wonder Wander" by Lenore Kandel from EPOS (Summer 1961).

Bruce Fearing for "Some Brown Sparrows" by Bruce Fearing from THE BEAT SCENE, ©1960 by Elias Wilentz and Fred McDarrah.

Thomas Hornsby Ferril for "Swallows" by Thomas Hornsby Ferril from *The Atlantic Monthly* (February 1964), ©1964 by The Atlantic Monthly Co., Boston, Mass.

Roland Flint for "August from My Desk" by Roland Flint from *The Atlantic Monthly* (February 1965), ©1965 by The Atlantic Monthly Co., Boston, Mass.

Folkways Music Publishers, Inc. for "Grey Goose" words and music by Huddie Ledbetter. Collected and adapted by John A. Lomax & Alan Lomax, copyright 1936, © renewed 1964 Folkways Music Publishers, Inc., New York, N. Y.

Robert Francis for "Preparation" and "Summons" from THE SOUND I LISTENED FOR by Robert Francis, copyright 1944 by Robert Francis. Published by The Macmillan Co.

Donald Hall for "Transcontinent" by Donald Hall from *Saturday Review*, April 11, 1959, ©1959 by *Saturday Review*.

Harcourt, Brace & World, Inc. for "Arithmetic" from COMPLETE POEMS, copyright 1950 by Carl Sandburg; "Fueled" from SERVE ME A SLICE OF THE MOON, ©1965 by Marcie Hans; "in Just-," copyright 1923, 1951 by E. E. Cummings. Reprinted from his volume, POEMS 1923-1954; "To Look at Any Thing," ©1961 by John Moffitt. Reprinted from his volume, THE LIVING SEED.

Harper & Row, Publishers for "Sunning" from A WORLD TO KNOW by James S. Tippett, copyright 1933 by Harper & Row, Publishers, renewed 1961 by Martha K. Tippett.

Hastings House, Publishers, Inc. for "Advice to Travelers" from COME AS YOU ARE, ©1958 by Walker Gibson. Originally appeared in *Saturday Review*.

Curtis Heath for "Wild Goose" by Curtis Heath from *The Saturday Evening Post*, ©1958 The Curtis Publishing Co.

Ruth Herschberger for "The Bat" by Ruth Herschberger from *Poetry Magazine* (April 1951), copyright 1951 by Ruth Herschberger.

Carl Wendell Hines, Jr. for "Two Jazz Poems" by Carl Wendell Hines, Jr. from AMERICAN NEGRO POETRY, ©1963 by Carl Wendell Hines, Jr. Published by Hill and Wang, Inc.

Edwin A. Hoey for "Foul Shot" by Edwin A. Hoey, which appeared in *READ* Magazine, published by Wesleyan University Press, Inc. An American Education Publication, Education Center, Columbus, Ohio. ©1962 by *READ* Magazine.

Holt, Rinehart and Winston, Inc. for "Lost" from CHICAGO POEMS by Carl Sandburg, copyright 1916 by Holt, Rinehart and Winston, Inc., copyright 1944 by Carl Sandburg; "A Patch of Old Snow" from COMPLETE POEMS OF ROBERT FROST, copyright 1916 by Holt, Rinehart and Winston, Inc., copyright 1944 by Robert Frost; "Steam Shovel" from UPPER PASTURE by Charles Malam, copyright 1930, ©1958 by Charles Malam.

Indiana University Press for "Fireworks" from COLLECTED POEMS: 1919-1962 by Babette Deutsch. First appeared in *The New Yorker*, October 20, 1962.

Beatrice Janosco for "The Garden Hose" by Beatrice Janosco, ©1966 by Scott, Foresman and Co.

Sy Kahn for "Boy with Frogs" by Sy Kahn from OUR SEPARATE DARKNESS; "Giraffes" by Sy Kahn from TRIPTICH.

Freda Quenneville for "Mother's Biscuits" by Freda Quenneville from *The Western Humanities Review* (Winter 1965).

Random House, Inc. for "Interlude III" from POEMS 1940-1953 by Karl Shapiro, copyright 1944 by Karl Shapiro.

The Ben Roth Agency, Inc. for "Hey Diddle Diddle" and "Little Miss Muffet" from RHYMES FOR A MODERN NURSERY by Paul Dehn, © Punch, London.

Sydney King Russell for "Dust" from SELECTED POEMS, copyright 1949 by Sydney King Russell. Published by House of Falmouth, Inc.

Mrs. Lew Sarett for "Four Little Foxes" from COVENANT WITH EARTH by Lew Sarett. Edited and copyrighted 1956 by Alma Johnson Sarett and published by the University of Florida Press, Gainesville.

Scholastic Magazines, Inc. for "Carmel Point" by Margaret Phyllis MacSweeney; "Husbands and Wives" by Miriam Hershenson; "Loneliness" by Brooks Jenkins; "War" by Dan Roth; copyright 1930, 1934, 1935, 1963 by Scholastic Magazines, Inc.

Winfield Townley Scott for "Two Lives and Others" from COLLECTED POEMS 1937-1962 (Macmillan Co.) copyright 1955, 1959 by Winfield Townley Scott.

Charles Scribner's Sons for "Earth" from THE BASHFUL EARTHQUAKE by Oliver Herford; "Earth" from THE GARDENER AND OTHER POEMS by John Hall Wheelock, ©1961 by John Hall Wheelock; "Hunting Song," ©1955 Pocket Books, Inc., from *The Clothing's New Emperor and Other Poems* by Donald Finkel, POETS OF TODAY VI; "Southbound on the Freeway," ©1963 May Swenson from TO MIX WITH TIME by May Swenson. First appeared in *The New Yorker*.

The Society of Authors, representatives of The Literary Trustees of Walter de la Mare for "Bones" from STUFF AND NONSENSE by Walter de la Mare.

William Stafford for "Fifteen" by William Stafford from *The Atlantic Monthly* (February 1964), ©1964 by The Atlantic Monthly Co.

Alan Swallow, Publisher for "April" from COLLECTED POEMS by Ivor Winters.

Robert L. Tyler for "Puppy" from THE DEPOSITION OF DON QUIXOTE AND OTHER POEMS by Robert L. Tyler, published by Golden Quill Press.

University of Nebraska Press for "The Forecast" by Dan Jaffe from *Prairie Schooner*, ©1964 by the University of Nebraska Press.

University of New Mexico Press for the following selections from *New Mexico Quarterly*: "Absolutes" by Gustave Keyser (Autumn 1963); "Reflections on a Gift of Watermelon Pickle Received from a Friend Called Felicity" by John Tobias (Spring 1961); "The Trap" by William Beyer (Autumn 1959). ©1963, 1961, 1959 by the University of New Mexico Press.

The Viking Press, Inc. for "Crossing" from LETTER FROM A DISTANT LAND by Philip Booth, copyright 1953 by Philip Booth. Originally appeared in *The New Yorker*; "Reflections Dental" from TIMES THREE by Phyllis McGinley, copyright © 1957 by Phyllis McGinley. Originally appeared in *The New Yorker*; "Resume" by Dorothy Parker, from THE PORTABLE DOROTHY PARKER, copyright 1926, 1954 by Dorothy Parker; "The Stump" from A ROOF OF TIGER LILIES by Donald Hall, copyright © 1964 by Donald Hall

Wesleyan University Press for "The Base Stealer" from THE ORB WEAVER, copyright 1948 by Robert Francis.

PHOTO CREDITS: Page 12: Ben F. Laposky. Page 18: James Ballard. Page 32: Harry M. Callahan. Page 48: Ferenc Berko. Pages 24, 38, 80, 106, 116, 132: H. Armstrong Roberts. Page 62: H. Anne Plettinger. Page 70: Photo/Wallowitch. Page 88: David Attie. Page 96: Donald Stebbing. Page 124: James H. Karales.

CONTENTS

SECTION 5

SECTION 6

SECTION 7

SECTION 8

Unfolding Bud

One is amazed
By a water-lily bud
Unfolding
With each passing day,
Taking on a richer color
And new dimensions.

One is not amazed,
At a first glance,
By a poem,
Which is as tight-closed
As a tiny bud.

Yet one is surprised
To see the poem
Gradually unfolding,
Revealing its rich inner self,
As one reads it
Again
And over again.

Naoshi Koriyama

Gone Forever

Halfway through shaving, it came—
the word for a poem.
I should have scribbled it
on the mirror with a soapy finger,
or shouted it to my wife in the kitchen,
or muttered it to myself till it ran
in my head like a tune.

But now it's gone with the whiskers
down the drain. Gone forever,
like the girls I never kissed,
and the places I never visited—
the lost lives I never lived.

Barriss Mills

To Look

at

Any Thing

To look at any thing,
If you would know that thing,
You must look at it long:
To look at this green and say
'I have seen spring in these
Woods,' will not do—you must
Be the thing you see:
You must be the dark snakes of
Stems and ferny plumes of leaves,
You must enter in
To the small silences between
The leaves,
You must take your time
And touch the very peace
They issue from.

John Moffitt

Poets Hitchhiking on the Highway

Of course I tried to tell him
but he cranked his head
     without an excuse.
I told him the sky chases
     the sun
And he smiled and said:
     "What's the use."
I was feeling like a demon
     again
So I said: "But the ocean chases
     the fish."
This time he laughed
     and said: "Suppose the
          strawberry were
               pushed into a mountain."

After that I knew the
    war was on—
So we fought:
He said: "The apple-cart like a
              broomstick-angel
        snaps & splinters
              old dutch shoes."
I said: "Lightning will strike the old oak
       and free the fumes!"
He said: "Mad street with no name."
I said: "Bald killer! Bald killer! Bald killer!"
He said, getting real mad,
        "Firestoves! Gas! Couch!"
I said, only smiling,
        "I know God would turn back his head
        if I sat quietly and thought."
We ended by melting away,
    hating the air!

Gregory Corso

Absolutes

(From an ink painting by Seiho)

black on white
crow in snow
       hunched
       wet lump
on brittle branch
remembering warmth
remembering corn
miserable
as life
is
black on white

          Gustave Keyser

The Crows

I shortcut home between Wade's tipsy shocks,
And lookout crows alert in the bare elm
Ask each other about this form that walks
Stubbled mud they considered their own farm.
They know there's death and loss where such shapes go.
I have no gun—I even feel akin
To these rude, lively birds. But to a crow
Kinship means Crow, and I'm not of his clan.

Off they flap to the wood with a hoarse curse,
And though the landscape's greyer with them gone
I'm glad they're skeptics—someday someone else
Trudging these ruts may raise a sudden gun.
Distrust me, crow!—the not-as-crow-, the other.
Croak, 'Damn your eyes!', and call no man your brother.

Leah Bodine Drake

Crows

David McCord

I like to walk
And hear the black crows talk.

I like to lie
And watch crows sail the sky.

I like the crow
That wants the wind to blow:

I like the one
That thinks the wind is fun.

I like to see
Crows spilling from a tree,

And try to find
The top crow left behind.

I like to hear
Crows caw that spring is near.

I like the great
Wild clamor of crow hate

Three farms away
When owls are out by day.

I like the slow
Tired homeward-flying crow;

I like the sight
Of crows for my good night.

Some Brown Sparrows

Some brown sparrows who live
in the Bronx Zoo visit often
the captive Victoria Crested
Pheasant, visit captive Peacocks,
Cockatoos. They fly through bars
to visit also monkeys, jackals,
bears. They delouse themselves in
cage dust, shaking joyously;
they hunt for bread crumbs, seeds
or other tidbits. Briefly,
they lead free sparrow lives
and fly free.

Bruce Fearing

Swallows

The prairie wind blew harder than it could,
Even the spines of cactus trembled back,
I crouched in an arroyo clamping my hands
On my eyes the sand was stinging yellow black.

In a break of the black I let my lashes part,
Looked overhead and saw I was not alone,
I could almost reach through the roar and almost touch
A treadmill of swallows almost holding their own.

Thomas Hornsby Ferril

Why Nobody Pets the Lion at the Zoo

The morning that the world began
The Lion growled a growl at Man.

And I suspect the Lion might
(If he'd been closer) have tried a bite.

I think that's as it ought to be
And not as it was taught to me.

I think the Lion has a right
To growl a growl and bite a bite.

And if the Lion bothered Adam,
He should have growled right back at 'im.

The way to treat a Lion right
Is growl for growl and bite for bite.

True, the Lion is better fit
For biting than for being bit.

But if you look him in the eye
You'll find the Lion's rather shy.

He really wants someone to pet him.
The trouble is: his teeth won't let him.

He has a heart of gold beneath
But the Lion just can't trust his teeth.

John Ciardi

Seal

See how he dives
  From the rocks with a zoom!
   See how he darts
   Through his watery room
    Past crabs and eels
    And green seaweed,
    Past fluffs of sandy
   Minnow feed!
   See how he swims
   With a swerve and a twist,
  A flip of the flipper,
  A flick of the wrist!
  Quicksilver-quick,
 Softer than spray,
 Down he plunges
And sweeps away;
Before you can think,
Before you can utter
Words like "Dill pickle"
Or "Apple butter,"
Back up he swims
 Past sting-ray and shark,
  Out with a zoom,
  A whoop, a bark;
   Before you can say
   Whatever you wish,
    He plops at your side
     With a mouthful of fish!

William Jay Smith

Boy with Frogs

Under his relentless eye,
Jarred and jeered,
The small frogs hop
And pulse in their
Suddenly glass world.

He, blond and curious,
Captive and captivated,
Holds in his hands
World of water, pebbles, grass
And the power
Of topsy-turvy and crash.

But he is content
To study them a while,
With their delicate legs
Pressed against the glass,
The futile leaps to freedom
And their frantic eyes.

It's a game for a God
Of course.
Later, the vibrant frogs,
Still leaping with protest
And life, are forgotten
On a shelf. He is out
Wondering about the waterbugs.

Sy Kahn

Giraffes

Stilted creatures,
Features fashioned as a joke,
Boned and buckled,
Finger painted,

They stand in the field
On long-pronged legs
As if thrust there.
They airily feed,
Slightly swaying,
Like hammer-headed flowers.

Bizarre they are,
Built silent and high,
Ornaments against the sky.
Ears like leaves
To hear the silken
Brushing of the clouds.

Sy Kahn

Deer Hunt

Because the warden is a cousin, my
mountain friends hunt in summer when the deer
cherish each rattler-ridden spring, and I
have waited hours by a pool in fear
that manhood would require I shoot or that
the steady drip of the hill would dull my ear
to a snake whispering near the log I sat
upon, and listened to the yelping cheer
of dogs and men resounding ridge to ridge.
I flinched at every lonely rifle crack,
my knuckles whitening where I gripped the edge
of age and clung, like retching, sinking back,
then gripping once again the monstrous gun—
since I, to be a man, had taken one.

Judson Jerome

The Bat

Being a mammal, I have less care than birds,
Being a flight-borne creature, need no home,
So while the beaver builds its, robin its nest,
I hook my hind feet into a wall or ceiling
And hang there looking at the world made silly
By being turned around and upside-down.
Sleep, sleep is my nourishment, I sleep
All day, all winter, and my young's but one.
At first I fly with it at my breast, even hunting,
But if it bores me I hang it on a wall
And go alone, enjoying insects frankly.
Tons, tons, I devour tons of insects, half
Of my weight is insects eaten within one night,
Yet cleverer than the swift or swallow, I deploy
Twist, turn, dodge, catch mosquitoes one by one.
And if the human family finds me odd,
No odder they, locked in their crazy yards.

Ruth Herschberger

The Bat

By day the bat is cousin to the mouse.
He likes the attic of an aging house.

His fingers make a hat about his head.
His pulse beat is so slow we think him dead.

He loops in crazy figures half the night
Among the trees that face the corner light.

But when he brushes up against a screen,
We are afraid of what our eyes have seen:

For something is amiss or out of place
When mice with wings can wear a human face.

Theodore Roethke

SECTION FOUR

Apartment House

A filing-cabinet of human lives
Where people swarm like bees in tunneled hives,
Each to his own cell in the towered comb,
Identical and cramped—we call it home.

Gerald Raftery

The Toaster

A silver-scaled Dragon with jaws flaming red
Sits at my elbow and toasts my bread.
I hand him fat slices, and then, one by one,
He hands them back when he sees they are done.

                    William Jay Smith

On Watching the Construction
of a Skyscraper

Nothing sings from these orange trees,
Rindless steel as smooth as sapling skin,
Except a crane's brief wheeze
And all the muffled, clanking din
Of rivets nosing in like bees.

                              Burton Raffel

Steam Shovel

The dinosaurs are not all dead.
I saw one raise its iron head
To watch me walking down the road
Beyond our house today.
Its jaws were dripping with a load
Of earth and grass that it had cropped.
It must have heard me where I stopped,
Snorted white steam my way,
And stretched its long neck out to see,
And chewed, and grinned quite amiably.

Charles Malam

The Builders

I told them a thousand times if I told them once:
Stop fooling around, I said, with straw and sticks;
They won't hold up; you're taking an awful chance.
Brick is the stuff to build with, solid bricks.
You want to be impractical, go ahead.
But just remember, I told them; wait and see.
You're making a big mistake. Awright, I said,
But when the wolf comes, don't come running to me.

The funny thing is, they didn't. There they sat,
One in his crummy yellow shack, and one
Under his roof of twigs, and the wolf ate
Them, hair and hide. Well, what is done is done.
But I'd been willing to help them, all along,
If only they'd once admitted they were wrong.

Sara Henderson Hay

SECTION FIVE

August from My Desk

It is hot today, dry enough for cutting grain,
and I am drifting back to North Dakota
where butterflies are all gone brown with wheat dust.

And where some boy,
red-faced, sweating, chafed,
too young to be dying this way
steers a laborious, self-propelled combine,
and dreams of cities, and blizzards—
and airplanes.

With the white silk scarf of his sleeve
he shines and shines his goggles,
he checks his meters, checks his flaps,
screams contact at his dreamless father,
and, engines roaring,
he pulls back the stick

and hurtles into the sun.

Roland Flint

Kansas Boy

This Kansas boy who never saw the sea
Walks through the young corn rippling at his knee
As sailors walk; and when the grain grows higher
Watches the dark waves leap with greener fire
Than ever oceans hold. He follows ships,
Tasting the bitter spray upon his lips,
For in his blood up-stirs the salty ghost
Of one who sailed a storm-bound English coast.
Across wide fields he hears the sea winds crying,
Shouts at the crows—and dreams of white gulls flying.

Ruth Lechlitner

Crossing Kansas by Train

Donald Justice

*The telephone poles
have been holding their
arms out
a long time now
to birds
that will not
settle there
but pass with
strange cawings
westward to
where dark trees
gather about
a waterhole. This
is Kansas. The
mountains start here
just behind
the closed eyes
of a farmer's
sons asleep
in their workclothes.*

Advice to Travelers

A burro once, sent by express,
His shipping ticket on his bridle,
Ate up his name and his address,
And in some warehouse, standing idle,
He waited till he like to died.
The moral hardly needs the showing:
Don't keep things locked up deep inside—
Say who you are and where you're going.

Walker Gibson

Transcontinent

Where the cities end, the
dumps grow the oil-can shacks
from Portland, Maine,

to Seattle. Broken
cars rust in Troy, New York,
and Cleveland Heights.

On the train, the people
eat candy bars, and watch,
or fall asleep.

When they look outside and
see cars and shacks, they know
they're nearly there.

Donald Hall

Crossing

STOP   LOOK   LISTEN
 as gate stripes swing down,
  count the cars hauling distance
  upgrade through town:
  warning whistle, bellclang,
   engine eating steam,
   engineer waving,
   a fast-freight dream:
   B&M boxcar,
    boxcar again,
    Frisco gondola,
eight-nine-ten,
 Erie and Wabash,
 Seaboard, U.P.,
 Pennsy tankcar,
twenty-two, three,
 Phoebe Snow, B&O,
thirty-four, five,
 Santa Fe cattle
  shipped alive,
   red cars, yellow cars,

orange cars, black,
Youngstown steel
down to Mobile
on Rock Island track,
fifty-nine, sixty,
hoppers of coke,
Anaconda copper,
hotbox smoke,
eighty-eight,
red-ball freight,
Rio Grande,
Nickel Plate,
Hiawatha,
Lackawanna,
rolling fast
and loose,
ninety-seven,
coal car,
boxcar,
CABOOSE!

Philip Booth

African Sunrise

Sky
Over the last star;
The parrot-winds
Sharp-beaked with yellow
Nipping the bunched date palms . . .

Now the camels
Open their beeswax eyes
And raise long necks,
Rutted sound in their throats—
Camels, pock-marking the sand with spread knees,
Lifting the odor of under-body with them.

Sun—
The burn of it
Hot-coined to each eyelid,
And desert-stretched,
        the caravan of hours
            not yet begun.

Gertrude May Lutz

Central
Park
Tourney

Mildred Weston

Cars
In the Park
With long spear lights
Ride at each other
Like armored knights;
Rush,
Miss the mark,
Pierce the dark,
Dash by!
Another two
Try.

Staged
In the Park
From dusk
To dawn,
The tourney goes on:
Rush,
Miss the mark,
Pierce the dark,
Dash by!
Another two
Try.

Reflections Dental

How pure, how beautiful, how fine
Do teeth on television shine!
No flutist flutes, no dancer twirls,
But comes equipped with matching pearls.
Gleeful announcers all are born
With sets like rows of hybrid corn.
Clowns, critics, clergy, commentators,
Ventriloquists and roller skaters,
M.C.s who beat their palms together,
The girl who diagrams the weather,
The crooner crooning for his supper—
All flash white treasures, lower and upper.
With miles of smiles the airwaves teem,
And each an orthodontist's dream.

'Twould please my eye as gold a miser's—
One charmer with uncapped incisors.

                    Phyllis McGinley

Arithmetic

Arithmetic is where numbers fly like pigeons in and out of your
     head.
Arithmetic tells you how many you lose or win if you know how
     many you had before you lost or won.
Arithmetic is seven eleven all good children go to heaven—or five
     six bundle of sticks.
Arithmetic is numbers you squeeze from your head to your hand
     to your pencil to your paper till you get the answer.
Arithmetic is where the answer is right and everything is nice and
     you can look out of the window and see the blue sky—or the
     answer is wrong and you have to start all over and try again
     and see how it comes out this time.

*If you take a number and double it and double it again and then
double it a few more times, the number gets bigger and bigger
and goes higher and higher and only arithmetic can tell you
what the number is when you decide to quit doubling.*

*Arithmetic is where you have to multiply—and you carry the
multiplication table in your head and hope you won't lose it.*

*If you have two animal crackers, one good and one bad, and you
eat one and a striped zebra with streaks all over him eats the
other, how many animal crackers will you have if somebody
offers you five six seven and you say No no no and you say
Nay nay nay and you say Nix nix nix?*

*If you ask your mother for one fried egg for breakfast and she
gives you two fried eggs and you eat both of them, who is
better in arithmetic, you or your mother?*

Carl Sandburg

Wonder Wander

in the afternoon the children walk like ducks
like geese
like from here to there
eyeing bird-trees puppy dogs candy windows
sun balls ice cream wagons
lady bugs rose bushes fenced yards vacant lots
tall buildings
and other things
big business men take big business walks
wear big business clothes
carry big business briefcases talk about
big business affairs in
big business voices
young girls walk pretty on the streets
stroll the avenues linger by
shop windows wedding rings lady hats
shiny dresses fancy shoes
whisper like turkey hens passing the time
young men stride on parade dream headed
wild eyed eating up the world
with deep glances rubbing empty fingers
in their empty pockets and
planning
me, I wander around soft-shoed easy-legged
watching the scene as it goes
finding things sea-gull feathers pink baby roses
every time I see a letter on the sidewalk
I stop and look it might be
        for me

Lenore Kandel

52

The Microscope

Anton Leeuwenhoek was Dutch.
He sold pincushions, cloth, and such.
The waiting townsfolk fumed and fussed
As Anton's dry goods gathered dust.

He worked, instead of tending store,
At grinding special lenses for
A microscope. Some of the things
He looked at were:
                        mosquitoes' wings,
the hairs of sheep, the legs of lice,
the skin of people, dogs, and mice;
ox eyes, spiders' spinning gear,
fishes' scales, a little smear
of his own blood,
                  and best of all,
the unknown, busy, very small
bugs that swim and bump and hop
inside a simple water drop.

Impossible! Most Dutchmen said.
This Anton's crazy in the head.
We ought to ship him off to Spain.
He says he's seen a housefly's brain.
He says the water that we drink
Is full of bugs. He's mad, we think!

They called him dumkopf, which means dope.
That's how we got the microscope.

                                    Maxine Kumin

Summons

Keep me from going to sleep too soon
Or if I go to sleep too soon
Come wake me up. Come any hour
Of night. Come whistling up the road.
Stomp on the porch. Bang on the door.
Make me get out of bed and come
And let you in and light a light.
Tell me the northern lights are on
And make me look. Or tell me clouds
Are doing something to the moon
They never did before, and show me.
See that I see. Talk to me till
I'm half as wide awake as you
And start to dress wondering why
I ever went to bed at all.
Tell me the walking is superb.
Not only tell me but persuade me.
You know I'm not too hard persuaded.

                    Robert Francis

Margaret mentioned Indians,
And I began to think about Indians—

Indians once living
Where now we are living—

Indians And I thought how little I know
About Indians. Oh, I know

What I have heard. Not much,
John When I think how much
Fandel

I wonder about them,
When a mere mention of them,

Indians, *starts me. I*
Think of their wigwams. I

Think of canoes. I think
Of quick arrows. I think

Of things Indian. And still
I think of their bright, still

Summers, when these hills
And meadows on these hills

Shone in the morning
Suns before this morning.

Loneliness

I was about to go, and said so;
And I had almost started for the door.
But he was all alone in the sugar-house,
And more lonely than he'd ever been before.
We'd talked for half an hour, almost,
About the price of sugar, and how I like my school,
And he had made me drink some syrup hot,
Telling me it was better that way than when cool.

And I agreed, and thanked him for it,
And said good-bye, and was about to go.
Want to see where I was born?
He asked me quickly. How to say no?

The sugar-house looked over miles of valley.
He pointed with a sticky finger to a patch of snow
Where he was born. The house, he said, was gone.
I can understand these people better, now I know.

Brooks Jenkins

Child

on Top

of a

Greenhouse

The wind billowing out the seat of my britches,
My feet crackling splinters of glass and dried putty,
The half-grown chrysanthemums staring up like accusers,
Up through the streaked glass, flashing with sunlight,
A few white clouds all rushing eastward,
A line of elms plunging and tossing like horses,
And everyone, everyone pointing up and shouting!

Theodore Roethke

Husbands

and

Wives

Husbands and wives
   With children between them
Sit in the subway;
   So I have seen them.

One word only
   From station to station;
So much talk for
   So close a relation.

Miriam Hershenson

This Is Just to Say

*I have eaten
the plums
that were in
the icebox*

*and which
you were probably
saving
for breakfast*

*Forgive me
they were delicious
so sweet
and so cold.*

William Carlos Williams

The Ne'er-Do-Well

Arthur M. Sampley

When Enoch should have been at work,
He might be fishing in the creek,
Or when the dewberries were ripe,
He'd leave his plowing for a week.
He'd take an hour to smoke a pipe,
Sitting with legs crossed like a Turk.

And yet the banker, looking grim
When Enoch with a note past due
Had left his corn patch to the cows,
Sought a persimmon grove he knew
And, finding Enoch in the boughs,
Stared long and wistfully at him.

Meditatio

When I carefully consider the curious habits of dogs
I am compelled to conclude
That man is the superior animal.

When I consider the curious habits of man
I confess, my friend, I am puzzled.

Ezra Pound

Ancient History

Arthur Guiterman

*I hope the old Romans
Had painful abdomens.*

*I hope that the Greeks
Had toothache for weeks.*

*I hope the Egyptians
Had chronic conniptions.*

*I hope that the Arabs
Were bitten by scarabs.*

*I hope that the Vandals
Had thorns in their sandals.*

*I hope that the Persians
Had gout in all versions.*

*I hope that the Medes
Were kicked by their steeds.*

*They started the fuss
And left it to us!*

Rebecca

Who slammed Doors for Fun and Perished Miserably

A Trick that everyone abhors
In Little Girls is slamming Doors.
A Wealthy Banker's little Daughter
Who lived in Palace Green, Bayswater
(By name Rebecca Offendort),
Was given to this Furious Sport.
She would deliberately go
And Slam the door like Billy-Ho!
To make her Uncle Jacob start.
She was not really bad at heart,
But only rather rude and wild:
She was an aggravating child.

It happened that a Marble Bust
Of Abraham was standing just
Above the Door this little Lamb
Had carefully prepared to Slam,
And down it came! It knocked her flat!
It laid her out! She looked like that!

  • • • • • • • • •

Her funeral Sermon (which was long
And followed by a Sacred Song)
Mentioned her Virtues, it is true,
But dwelt upon her Vices too,
And showed the Dreadful End of One
Who goes and slams the door for Fun.

Hilaire Belloc

Nymph, nymph, what are your beads?

Green glass, goblin. Why do you stare at them?

Give them me.

        No.

Give them me. Give them me.

           No.

Then I will howl all night in the reeds,
Lie in the mud and howl for them.

Goblin, why do you love them so?

They are better than stars or water,
Better than voices of winds that sing,
Better than any man's fair daughter,
Your green glass beads on a silver ring.

Hush, I stole them out of the moon.

Give me your beads, I want them.

           No.

I will howl in a deep lagoon
For your green glass beads, I love them so.
Give them me. Give them.

        No.

Dust

Agatha Morley
All her life
Grumbled at dust
Like a good wife.

Dust on a table,
Dust on a chair,
Dust on a mantel
She couldn't bear.

She forgave faults
In man and child
But a dusty shelf
Would set her wild.

She bore with sin
Without protest,
But dust thoughts preyed
Upon her rest.

Agatha Morley
Is sleeping sound
Six feet under
The mouldy ground.

Six feet under
The earth she lies
With dust at her feet
And dust in her eyes.

Sydney King Russell

Bones

Said Mr. Smith, "I really cannot
  Tell you, Dr. Jones—
The most peculiar pain I'm in—
  I think it's in my bones."

Said Dr. Jones, "Oh, Mr. Smith,
  That's nothing. Without doubt
We have a simple cure for that;
  It is to take them out."

He laid forthwith poor Mr. Smith
  Close-clamped upon the table,
And, cold as stone, took out his bone
  As fast as he was able.

And Smith said, "Thank you, thank you, thank you,"
  And wished him a good-day;
And with his parcel 'neath his arm
  He slowly moved away.

Walter de la Mare

On the Vanity of Earthly Greatness

Arthur Guiterman

The tusks that clashed in mighty brawls
Of mastodons, are billiard balls.

The sword of Charlemagne the Just
Is ferric oxide, known as rust.

The grizzly bear whose potent hug
Was feared by all, is now a rug.

Great Caesar's dead and on the shelf,
And I don't feel so well myself!

Résumé

Razors pain you;
Rivers are damp;
Acids stain you;
And drugs cause cramp.
Guns aren't lawful;
Nooses give;
Gas smells awful;
You might as well live.

Dorothy Parker

Too Blue

I got those sad old weary blues.
I don't know where to turn.
I don't know where to go.
Nobody cares about you
When you sink so low.

What shall I do?
What shall I say?
Shall I take a gun and
Put myself away?

I wonder if
One bullet would do?
Hard as my head is,
It would probably take two.

But I ain't got
Neither bullet nor gun—
And I'm too blue
To look for one.

Langston Hughes

Fifteen   *South of the Bridge on Seventeenth*
I found back of the willows one summer
day a motorcycle with engine running
as it lay on its side, ticking over
slowly in the high grass. I was fifteen.

I admired all that pulsing gleam, the
shiny flanks, the demure headlights
fringed where it lay; I led it gently
to the road and stood with that
companion, ready and friendly. I was fifteen.

We could find the end of a road, meet
the sky on out Seventeenth. I thought about
hills, and patting the handle got back a
confident opinion. On the bridge we indulged
a forward feeling, a tremble. I was fifteen.

Thinking, back farther in the grass I found
the owner, just coming to, where he had flipped
over the rail. He had blood on his hand, was pale—
I helped him walk to his machine. He ran his hand
over it, called me good man, roared away.

I stood there, fifteen.

William Stafford

Interlude III   Writing, I crushed an insect with my nail
And thought nothing at all. A bit of wing
Caught my eye then, a gossamer so frail

And exquisite, I saw in it a thing
That scorned the grossness of the thing I wrote.
It hung upon my finger like a sting.

A leg I noticed next, fine as a mote,
"And on this frail eyelash he walked," I said,
"And climbed and walked like any mountain-goat."

And in this mood I sought the little head,
But it was lost; then in my heart a fear
Cried out, "A life—why beautiful, why dead!"

It was a mite that held itself most dear,
So small I could have drowned it with a tear.

Karl Shapiro

Lost

Desolate and lone
All night long on the lake
Where fog trails and mist creeps,
The whistle of a boat
Calls and cries unendingly,
Like some lost child
In tears and trouble
Hunting the harbor's breast
And the harbor's eyes.

Carl Sandburg

War

Dawn came slowly,
almost not at all.
The sun crept over the hill
cautiously
fearful of being hit
by mortar fire.

Dan Roth

The Term

William Carlos Williams

A rumpled sheet
of brown paper
about the length

and apparent bulk
of a man was
rolling with the

wind slowly over
and over in
the street as

a car drove down
upon it and
crushed it to

the ground. Unlike
a man it rose
again rolling

with the wind over
and over to be as
it was before.

A Coney Island Life

Having lived a Coney Island life
on rollercoaster ups and downs
and seen my helium hopes
break skyward without me,
now arms filled with dolls
I threw so much for
I take perhaps my last ride
on this planet-carousel
and ask
how many more times round
I have
to catch that brass-ring-sun
before the game is up.

James L. Weil

from **Two Jazz Poems**

yeah here am i
am standing
at the crest of a tallest
hill with a trumpet
in my hand & dark
glasses
on.
      bearded & bereted i proudly stand!
         but there are no eyes to see me.
      i send down cool sounds!
         but there are no ears to hear me.

          Carl Wendell Hines, Jr.

Carmel Point

I watched a sea anemone
The color of green jade
Shadowed under water.

I saw a daring crab,
Unafraid and young
Touch the velvet petals
Of that princess under water.
Softly she took him in,
Softly she sighed and closed.
The little crab was hushed and still—
Never would he swim again
Under crevice, under weed,
Under green and colored water.

Softly she opened—
That princess of rare jade.
Softly she gave him back
Sucked of all his pearly flesh
Sucked of all his salty blood.

I ran away to tell my dad,
"Let's go home," I said,
"I am sorry to be born,
I am afraid of many things."

Margaret Phyllis MacSweeney

Forgive My Guilt

Not always sure what things called sins may be,
I am sure of one sin I have done.
It was years ago, and I was a boy,
I lay in the frostflowers with a gun,
The air ran blue as the flowers, I held my breath,
Two birds on golden legs slim as dream things
Ran like quicksilver on the golden sand,
My gun went off, they ran with broken wings
Into the sea, I ran to fetch them in,
But they swam with their heads high out to sea,
They cried like two sorrowful high flutes,
With jagged ivory bones where wings should be.

For days I heard them when I walked that headland
Crying out to their kind in the blue,
The other plovers were going over south
On silver wings leaving these broken two.
The cries went out one day; but I still hear them
Over all the sounds of sorrow in war or peace
I ever have heard, time cannot drown them,
Those slender flutes of sorrow never cease.
Two airy things forever denied the air!
I never knew how their lives at last were spilt,
But I have hoped for years all that is wild,
Airy, and beautiful will forgive my guilt.

                    Robert P. Tristram Coffin

Sonic Boom

I'm sitting in the living room,
When, up above, the Thump of Doom
Resounds. Relax. It's sonic boom.

The ceiling shudders at the clap,
The mirrors tilt, the rafters snap,
And Baby wakens from his nap.

"Hush, babe. Some pilot we equip,
Giving the speed of sound the slip,
Has cracked the air like a penny whip."

Our world is far from frightening; I
No longer strain to read the sky
Where moving fingers (jet planes) fly.
Our world seems much too tame to die.

And if it does, with one more pop,
I shan't look up to see it drop.

John Updike

Southbound on the Freeway

A tourist came in from Orbitville,
parked in the air, and said:

The creatures of this star
are made of metal and glass.

Through the transparent parts
you can see their guts.

Their feet are round and roll
on diagrams or long

measuring tapes, dark
with white lines.

They have four eyes.
The two in back are red.

Sometimes you can see a five-eyed
one, with a red eye turning

on the top of his head.
He must be special—

the others respect him
and go slow

when he passes, winding
among them from behind.

They all hiss as they glide,
like inches, down the marked

tapes. Those soft shapes,
shadowy inside

the hard bodies—are they
their guts or their brains?

May Swenson

Earth
Oliver Herford

If this little world tonight
   Suddenly should fall through space
In a hissing, headlong flight,
   Shrivelling from off its face,
As it falls into the sun,
   In an instant every trace
Of the little crawling things—
   Ants, philosophers, and lice,
Cattle, cockroaches, and kings,
   Beggars, millionaires, and mice,
Men and maggots all as one
As it falls into the sun. . . .
Who can say but at the same
   Instant from some planet far
A child may watch us and exclaim:
   "See the pretty shooting star!"

Earth

*"A planet doesn't explode of itself," said drily
The Martian astronomer, gazing off into the air—
"That they were able to do it is proof that highly
Intelligent beings must have been living there."*

John Hall Wheelock

Fueled

Fueled
by a million
man-made
wings of fire—
the rocket tore a tunnel
through the sky—
and everybody cheered.
Fueled
only by a thought from God—
the seedling
urged its way
through the thicknesses of black—
and as it pierced
the heavy ceiling of the soil—
and launched itself
up into outer space—
no
one
even
clapped.

Marcie Hans

Little Miss Muffet

Little Miss Muffet
Crouched on a tuffet,
Collecting her shell-shocked wits.
There dropped (from a glider)
An H-bomb beside her—
Which frightened Miss Muffet to bits.

Paul Dehn

Hey Diddle Diddle

Hey diddle diddle,
The physicists fiddle,
The Bleep jumped over the moon.
The little dog laughed to see such fun
And died the following June.

Paul Dehn

On a Night of Snow

Cat, if you go outdoors you must walk in the snow.
You will come back with little white shoes on your feet,
Little white slippers of snow that have heels of sleet.
Stay by the fire, my Cat. Lie still, do not go.
See how the flames are leaping and hissing low.
I will bring you a saucer of milk like a marguerite,
So white and so smooth, so spherical and so sweet.
Stay with me, Cat. Outdoors the wild winds blow.

Outdoors the wild winds blow, Mistress, and dark is the night.
Strange voices cry in the trees, intoning strange lore,
And more than cats move, lit by our eyes' green light,
On silent feet where the meadow grasses hang hoar—
Mistress, there are portents abroad of magic and might,
And things that are yet to be done. Open the door!

Elizabeth Coatsworth

Catalogue

Cats sleep fat and walk thin.
Cats, when they sleep, slump;
When they wake, stretch and begin
Over, pulling their ribs in.
Cats walk thin.

Cats wait in a lump,
Jump in a streak.
Cats, when they jump, are sleek
As a grape slipping its skin—
They have technique.
Oh, cats don't creak.
They sneak.

Cats sleep fat.
They spread out comfort underneath them
Like a good mat,
As if they picked the place
And then sat;
You walk around one
As if he were the City Hall
After that.

If male,
A cat is apt to sing on a major scale;
This concert is for everybody, this
Is wholesale.
For a baton, he wields a tail.

(He is also found,
When happy, to resound
With an enclosed and private sound.)

A cat condenses.
He pulls in his tail to go under bridges,
And himself to go under fences.
Cats fit
In any size box or kit,
And if a large pumpkin grew under one,
He could arch over it.

When everyone else is just ready to go out,
The cat is just ready to come in.
He's not where he's been.
Cats sleep fat and walk thin.

                              Rosalie Moore

Poem

As the cat
climbed over
the top of

the jamcloset
first the right
forefoot

carefully
then the hind
stepped down

into the pit of
the empty
flowerpot.

William Carlos Williams

For a Dead Kitten

Put the rubber mouse away,
Pick the spools up from the floor,
What was velvet-shod, and gay,
Will not want them any more.

What was warm, is strangely cold.
Whence dissolved the little breath?
How could this small body hold
So immense a thing as Death?

Sara Henderson Hay

Unsatisfied Yearning

Down in the silent hallway
    Scampers the dog about,
And whines, and barks, and scratches,
    In order to get out.

Once in the glittering starlight,
    He straightway doth begin
To set up a doleful howling
    In order to get in!

                    Richard Kendall Munkittrick

Puppy

Catch and shake the cobra garden hose.
Scramble on panicky paws and flee
The hiss of tensing nozzle nose,
Or stalk that snobbish bee.

The back yard world is vast as park
With belly-tickle grass and stun
Of sudden sprinkler squalls that are
Rainbows to the yap yap sun.

                    Robert L. Tyler

Sunning

Old Dog lay in the summer sun
Much too lazy to rise and run.
He flapped an ear
At a buzzing fly.
He winked a half opened
Sleepy eye.
He scratched himself
On an itching spot,
As he dozed on the porch
Where the sun was hot.
He whimpered a bit
From force of habit
While he lazily dreamed
Of chasing a rabbit.
But Old Dog happily lay in the sun
Much too lazy to rise and run.

James S. Tippett

Elegy for Jog

Stiff-dog death, all froth on a bloody chin,
sniffs at the curb. Skinny-man death, his master,
opens the traffic's hedge to let him in.
Jog was his name, silliness his disaster.
He wasn't satisfied to scare the truck:
he had to bite the tire. Fools have no luck.

John Ciardi

Oz.

Whoever discounts
the ounce
as one of the smallest amounts
has never met up with the ounce
that belongs to the cat family.

This jungle ounce
will jounce
you out of complacency.
If you try to trounce
this ounce,
you will be chastened hastily;
for this ounce
does more than flounce;
this ounce can bounce,
this ounce can pounce.

So if you meet up with an ounce,
announce yourself as a friend,
or it might be The End.

P.S. Better not take a chounce.

Eve Merriam

SECTION ELEVEN

April   Marcia Masters

It's lemonade, it's lemonade, it's daisy.
It's a roller-skating, scissor-grinding day;
It's gingham-waisted, chocolate flavored, lazy,
With the children flower-scattered at their play.

It's the sun like watermelon,
And the sidewalks overlaid
With a glaze of yellow yellow
Like a jar of marmalade.

It's the mower gently mowing,
And the stars like startled glass,
While the mower keeps on going
Through a waterfall of grass.

Then the rich magenta evening
Like a sauce upon the walk,
And the porches softly swinging
With a hammockful of talk.

It's the hobo at the corner
With his lilac-sniffing gait,
And the shy departing thunder
Of the fast departing skate.

It's lemonade, it's lemonade, it's April!
A water sprinkler, puddle winking time,
When a boy who peddles slowly, with a smile remote and holy,
Sells you April chocolate flavored for a dime.

in Just-

E. E. Cummings

in Just-
spring   when the world is mud-
luscious the little
lame balloonman

whistles   far   and wee

and eddieandbill come
running from marbles and
piracies and it's
spring

when the world is puddle-wonderful

the queer
old balloonman whistles
far   and   wee
and bettyandisbel come dancing

from hop-scotch and jump-rope and

it's
spring
and
    the

           goat-footed

balloonMan   whistles
far
and
wee

The Child's Morning

Gangway for violets,
Old snow in the corner.
Sun after a rise of rain
Over cuttlebone cloud.
Sun in the brook running
Green with watercress
Sun on the spade—
We shovel out crocuses.
Up the concrete walk
Under surf of rollerskates
The hail of jacks,
Kiss-click of aggies.
We summon with jumpropes
Sap in the trees,
With bat-knock of ball
And the thudding glove.
That clang of schoolbells
We answer with answers:
Tall immaculate silence
Of colored kites.

Winfield Townley Scott

Four Little Foxes

Speak gently, Spring, and make no sudden sound;
For in my windy valley, yesterday I found
New-born foxes squirming on the ground—
              Speak gently.

Walk softly, March, forbear the bitter blow;
Her feet within a trap, her blood upon the snow,
The four little foxes saw their mother go—
              Walk softly.

Go lightly, Spring, oh, give them no alarm;
When I covered them with boughs to shelter them from harm,
The thin blue foxes suckled at my arm—
                Go lightly.

Step softly, March, with your rampant hurricane;
Nuzzling one another, and whimpering with pain,
The new little foxes are shivering in the rain—
                Step softly.

Lew Sarett

April

Yvor Winters

The little goat
crops
new grass lying down
leaps up eight inches
into air and
lands on four feet.
Not a tremor—
solid in the
spring and serious
he walks away.

Four Ducks on a Pond

William Allingham

Four ducks on a pond,
A grass-bank beyond,
A blue sky of spring,
White clouds on the wing;
What a little thing
To remember for years—
To remember with tears!

Swift Things Are Beautiful

Swift things are beautiful:
Swallows and deer,
And lightning that falls
Bright-veined and clear,
Rivers and meteors,
Wind in the wheat,
The strong-withered horse,
The runner's sure feet.

And slow things are beautiful:
The closing of day,
The pause of the wave
That curves downward to spray,
The ember that crumbles,
The opening flower,
And the ox that moves on
In the quiet of power.

Elizabeth Coatsworth

Counting-Out Rhyme

Silver bark of beech, and sallow
Bark of yellow birch and yellow
    Twig of willow.

Stripe of green in moosewood maple,
Colour seen in leaf of apple,
    Bark of popple.

Wood of popple pale as moonbeam,
Wood of oak for yoke and barn-beam,
    Wood of hornbeam.

Silver bark of beech, and hollow
Stem of elder, tall and yellow
    Twig of willow.

Edna St. Vincent Millay

SECTION TWELVE

Fish
    Story

Count this among my heartfelt wishes:
To hear a fish tale told by fishes
And stand among the fish who doubt
The honor of a fellow trout,
And watch the bulging of their eyes
To hear of imitation flies
And worms with rather droopy looks
Stuck through with hateful, horrid hooks,
And fishermen they fled all day from
(As big as this) and got away from.

              Richard Armour

Fortune

        Fortune
               has its cookies to give out

which is a good thing

            since it's been a long time since

      that summer in Brooklyn
    when they closed off the street
       one hot day
        and the

              FIREMEN

                    turned on their hoses

    and all the kids ran out in it

      in the middle of the street

    and there were

         maybe a couple dozen of us

              out there

with the water squirting up
                                to the

                        sky

                                        and all over
                                                us
            there was maybe only six of us
                                        kids altogether
                running around in our
                                        barefeet and birthday
                    suits
                        and I remember Molly but then

            the firemen stopped squirting their hoses
                all of a sudden and went
                    back in
                    their firehouse
                    and
                started playing pinochle again
                    just as if nothing
                        had ever
                                happened
        while I remember Molly
                        looked at me and

            ran in

        because I guess really we were the only ones there

                                Lawrence Ferlinghetti

Angler's Choice

H. J. Gottlieb

These he cast
Where the pool lay still
Under a lichened ledge:
Silver Doctor, Olive Quill,
Ibis, Lady Beaverkill,
    And a Dark Blue Sedge.

These he chose
For the stony flat
Spanned by the covered bridge:
Royal Coachman, Cahill, Gnat,
March Brown, Little Marryat,
    And a Berry Midge.

These he tried
In the fading light
Down by the alder thicket:
Yellow Sally, Sandy Mite,
Wickham's Fancy, Cocky Knight,
    And a real, live cricket.

The Fisher

Lyle Glazier

At half past four, mornings in June,
He met the sliding, whispery sound
Of Four Mile Brook, and liked the tune,
And liked the log road, morning-hushed;
His bare feet liked the dew-soaked ground.

At half past ten, he was headed for home,
Having tried his last last-hole for luck;
The heat and noise of the day had come,
But his bones were cool with the brookside shade,
And his ears kept the whirlpool's silvery suck.

Hunting

Song

The fox came lolloping, lolloping,
Lolloping. His tongue hung out
And his ears were high.
He was like death at the end of a string
When he came to the hollow
Log. Ran in one side
And out of the other. O
He was sly.

The hounds came tumbling, tumbling,
Tumbling. Their heads were low
And their eyes were red.
The sound of their breath was louder than death
When they came to the hollow
Log. They held at one end
But a bitch found the scent. O
They were mad.

The hunter came galloping, galloping,
Galloping. All damp was his mare
From her hooves to her mane.
His coat and his mouth were redder than death
When he came to the hollow
Log. He took in the rein
And over he went. O
He was fine.

The log, he just lay there, alone in
The clearing. No fox nor hound
Nor mounted man
Saw his black round eyes in their perfect disguise
(As the ends of a hollow
Log). He watched death go through him,
Around him, and over him. O
He was wise.

                              Donald Finkel

The Trap

"That red fox,
Back in the furthest field,
Caught in my hidden trap,
Was half mad with fear.
During the night
He must have ripped his foot
From the cold steel.
I saw him early this morning,
Dragging his hurt leg,
Bleeding a path across the gold wheat,
Whining with the pain;
His eyes like cracked marbles.
I followed as he moved,
His thin body pulled to one side
In a weird helplessness.
He hit the wire fence,
Pushing through it
Into the deep, morning corn,
And was gone."
The old man looked around the kitchen
To see if anyone was listening.
"Crazy red fox,

Will kill my chickens no longer.
Will die somewhere in hiding."
He lit the brown tobacco carefully,
Watching the blue smoke rise and disappear
In the movement of the air.
Scratching his red nose slowly,
Thinking something grave for a long moment,
He stared out of the bright window.
"He won't last long with that leg," he said.
The old man turned his head
To see if his wife was listening.
But she was deep in thought,
Her stained fingers
Pressing red berries in a pie.
He turned his white head
Toward the open window again.
"Guess I'll ride into the back field, first thing.
Some mighty big corn back there this year.
Mighty big corn."
His wife looked up from her work,
Smiled almost secretly to herself,
And finished packing the ripe berries
Into the pale crust.

William Beyer

With two 60's stuck on the scoreboard
And two seconds hanging on the clock,
The solemn boy in the center of eyes,
Squeezed by silence,
Seeks out the line with his feet,
Soothes his hands along his uniform,
Gently drums the ball against the floor,

Foul Shot

Then measures the waiting net,
Raises the ball on his right hand,
Balances it with his left,

Edwin A. Hoey

Calms it with fingertips,
Breathes,
Crouches,
Waits,
And then through a stretching of stillness,
Nudges it upward.

The ball
Slides up and out,
Lands,
Leans,
Wobbles,
Wavers,
Hesitates,
Exasperates,
Plays it coy
Until every face begs with unsounding screams—
And then

        And then

               And then,

Right before ROAR-UP,
Dives down and through.

Fireworks

Not guns, not thunder, but a flutter of clouded drums
That announce a fiesta: abruptly, fiery needles
Circumscribe on the night boundless chrysanthemums.
Softly, they break apart, they flake away, where
Darkness, on a svelte hiss, swallows them.
Delicate brilliance: a bellflower opens, fades,
In a sprinkle of falling stars.
Night absorbs them
With the sponge of her silence.

Babette Deutsch

The Base Stealer

Poised between going on and back, pulled
Both ways taut like a tightrope-walker,
Fingertips pointing the opposites,
Now bouncing tiptoe like a dropped ball
Or a kid skipping rope, come on, come on,
Running a scattering of steps sidewise,
How he teeters, skitters, tingles, teases,
Taunts them, hovers like an ecstatic bird,
He's only flirting, crowd him, crowd him,
Delicate, delicate, delicate, delicate—now!

Robert Francis

The Garden Hose

In the gray evening
I see a long green serpent
With its tail in the dahlias.

It lies in loops across the grass
And drinks softly at the faucet.

I can hear it swallow.

Beatrice Janosco

Lullaby

Robert Hillyer

The long canoe
Toward the shadowy shore,
One . . . two . . .
Three . . . four . . .
The paddle dips,
Turns in the wake,
Pauses, then
Forward again.
Water drips
From the blade to the lake.
Nothing but that,
No sound of wings;
The owl and bat
Are velvet things.
No wind awakes,
No fishes leap;
No rabbits creep
Among the brakes.
The long canoe
At the shadowy shore,
One . . . two . . .
Three . . . four . . .
A murmur now
Under the prow
Where rushes bow
To let us through.
One . . . two . . .
Upon the shore,
Three . . . four . . .
Upon the lake,
No one's awake,
No one's awake,
One . . . two . . .
No one, not even you.

Millions of Strawberries

Genevieve Taggard

Marcia and I went over the curve,
Eating our way down
Jewels of strawberries we didn't deserve,
Eating our way down.
Till our hands were sticky, and our lips painted,
And over us the hot day fainted,
And we saw snakes,
And got scratched,
And a lust overcame us for the red unmatched
Small buds of berries,
Till we lay down—
Eating our way down—
And rolled in the berries like two little dogs,
Rolled
In the late gold.
And gnats hummed,
And it was cold,
And home we went, home without a berry,
Painted red and brown,
Eating our way down.

Cheers

Eve Merriam

The frogs and the serpents each had a football team,
and I heard their cheer leaders in my dream:

"Bilgewater, bilgewater," called the frog,
"Bilgewater, bilgewater,
Sis, boom, bog!
Roll 'em off the log,
Slog 'em in the sog,
Swamp'em, swamp'em,
Muck mire quash!"

"Sisyphus, Sisyphus," hissed the snake,
"Sibilant, syllabub,
Syllable-loo-ba-lay.
Scylla and Charybdis,
Sumac, asphodel,
How do you spell Success?
With an S-S-S!"

The Forecast

Perhaps our age has driven us indoors.
We sprawl in the semi-darkness, dreaming sometimes
Of a vague world spinning in the wind.
But we have snapped our locks, pulled down our shades,
Taken all precautions. We shall not be disturbed.
If the earth shakes, it will be on a screen;
And if the prairie wind spills down our streets
And covers us with leaves, the weatherman will tell us.

Dan Jaffe

Mother's Biscuits

In a big bowl she'd fluff in flour,
Make a fist-dent
For buttermilk and lard which she squeezed
Between her fingers
The way a child goes at a mud puddle,
Raking dry flour
From the sides until it mixed right.

She'd give the dough a pat for luck,
Nip a springy bud,
Roll it round and flat-it-down
With a motion
Continued to a grease-shined pan.
Mother's biscuits
Cooked high, crusty, with succulent middles
That took attention
At company dinners; but on kitchen-nights
They were finest
Soaked with pot liquor or gravy.

And those rich biscuits could put a shine
On Sunday patent
That let the Lord know who was there.
A panful stood
Ready as magic at dawn's light:
I'd take some
When leaving late to the schoolbus
And up the road
I'd run, puffing through biscuit crumbs
My haloed breath
Into the skin-sharp morning air.

Freda Quenneville

Two Lives and Others

Beyond the field where crows cawed at a hawk
The road bent down between oaks, pines, and maples:
Maples skimming the air with terra cotta.
The oaks spat acorns over scurries of squirrels.
Moss crunched stiff underfoot, and overhead
The sky was gradually freezing, white across blue.
We hurried our walk through shadows, yet it was
A noticeable sort of afternoon:
We honored a faded robin and considered
The importance of the color gray on bluejays.
A woodchuck, all an urgent clumsiness,
Made his tumbling run, then he saw us,
Plunged, hid, and screamed his whistle of fear.
Round the next bend to twilight we went past
A solitary house, one room lamplighted,
An old man at supper alone facing the wall.
If he was aware of us he gave no sign.
We circled home, that last day before snow.

Winfield Townley Scott

The Pheasant

A pheasant cock sprang into view,
A living jewel, up he flew.

His wings laid hold on empty space,
Scorn bulged his eyeballs out with grace.

He was a hymn from tail to beak
With not a tender note or meek.

Then the gun let out its thunder,
The bird descended struck with wonder.

He ran a little, then, amazed,
Settled with his head upraised.

The fierceness flowed out of his eyes
And left them meek and large and wise.

Gentleness relaxed his head,
He lay in jewelled feathers, dead.

                    Robert P. Tristram Coffin

Fall

The geese flying south
In a row long and V-shaped
Pulling in winter.

Sally Andresen

November Day

Old haggard wind has
    plucked the trees
Like pheasants, held
    between her knees.
In rows she hangs them,
    bare and neat,
Their brilliant plumage at
    her feet.

Eleanor Averitt

Grey Goose

It was one Sunday mornin'
  Lawd, lawd, lawd![1]
The preacher went a-huntin'!
He carried 'long his shotgun.
Well, 'long come a grey goose.
The gun went off boo-loo
And down come a grey goose.
He was six weeks a-fallin'!
And my wife and yo' wife,
They give him feather-pickin'.
They was six weeks a-pickin',
And they put him on to parboil.
He was six weeks a boilin',
And they put him on the table,
And the knife wouldn't cut him,
Aw, the fork wouldn't stick him.
And they throwed him in the hog-pen,
And the hog couldn't eat him,
Aw, he broke the hog's teeth out.
They tak'n him to the saw mill,
And the saw wouldn't cut him.
Aw, he broke the saw's teeth out.
An' the last time I seed him,
He was flyin' cross de ocean
With a long string o' goslin's.
An' they all goin', "Quack, quack."

[1]This response follows each line.

                              Huddie Ledbetter

Wild Goose

He climbs the wind above
green clouds of pine,
Honking to hail the
gathering migration,
And, arching toward the
south, pulls to align
His flight into the great
spearhead formation.

He'll find a bayou land of
hidden pools,
And bask amid lush fern
and water lily
Far from the frozen world
of earth-bound fools
Who, shivering, maintain
that geese are silly.

Curtis Heath

Dreams

Hold fast to dreams
For if dreams die
Life is a broken-winged bird
That cannot fly.

Hold fast to dreams
For when dreams go
Life is a barren field
Frozen with snow.

Langston Hughes

Twin Lakes Hunter

Last night a freezing cottontail
Slept just outside our outside door
And drew upon the heat that leaked
Through threshold from the floor.

Rex, the hunter told me so.
"Cold out," he said. "Some storm!"
He hoped the little fellow
Slept snug enough and warm.

He backed up to the Monarch range,
A-shiver in his mackinaw.
"I been outside an hour," he said.
"Take me a week to thaw."

"Snug, so you can shoot him later?"
He answered, "Please don't scold.
It's just I can't abide the thought
Of dying from the cold."

A. B. Guthrie, Jr.

The Stump

Today they cut down the oak.
Strong men climbed with ropes
in the brittle tree.
The exhaust of a gasoline saw
was blue in the branches.

It is February. The oak has been dead a year.
I remember the great sails of its branches
rolling out greenly, a hundred and twenty feet up,
and acorns thick on the lawn.
Nine cities of squirrels lived in that tree.
Today they run over the snow
squeaking their lamentation.

Yet I was happy that it was coming down.
"Let it come down!" I kept saying to myself
with a joy that was strange to me.
Though the oak was the shade of old summers,
I loved the guttural saw.

Donald Hall

Rodeo

Leathery, wry, and rough,
Jaw full of chaw, and slits
For eyes—this guy is tough.
He climbs the slatted fence,
Pulls himself atop and sits;
Tilts back his cowboy hat,
Stained with sweat below
The crown, and wipes a dirty
Sleeve across his brow;
Then pulls the hat down tight,
Caresses up its sides,
And spits into the dust
A benediction.

Gracelessly, his Brahma bull
Lunges into the chute
And swings a baleful
Eye around, irresolute.

Vision narrower still,
The man regards the beast.
There's weight enough to kill,
Bone and muscle fit at least
To jar a man apart.
The cowboy sniffs and hitches at
His pants. Himself all heart
And gristle, he watches as
The hands outside the chute
Prepare the sacrificial act.
Standing now, and nerving up,
He takes his final measure
Of the creature's awful back.

Then he moves. Swerving up
And into place, he pricks
The Brahma's bullish pride.

The gate swings free, and
Screams begin to sanctify
Their pitching, tortured ride.

                    Edward Lueders

Preparation   *Last fall I saw the farmer follow*
The plow that dug the long dark furrows
Between the hillslope and the hollow.

All winter long the land lay fallow.
The woodchuck slept within his burrow
And heard no hound or farm boy's hallow.

Tonight the rain drives its dark arrows
Deep in the soil, down to its marrow.
The arrows of the sun tomorrow.

Robert Francis

Valentine

Donald Hall

Chipmunks jump, and
Greensnakes slither.
Rather burst than
Not be with her.

Bluebirds fight, but
Bears are stronger.
We've got fifty
Years or longer.

Hoptoads hop, but
Hogs are fatter.
Nothing else but
Us can matter.

Oregon Winter

The rain begins. This is no summer rain,
Dropping the blotches of wet on the dusty road:
This rain is slow, without thunder or hurry:
There is plenty of time—there will be months of rain.
  Lost in the hills, the old gray farmhouses
Hump their backs against it, and smoke from their chimneys
Struggles through weighted air. The sky is sodden with water,
It sags against the hills, and the wild geese,
Wedge-flying, brush the heaviest cloud with their wings.
  The farmers move unhurried. The wood is in,
The hay has long been in, the barn lofts piled
Up to the high windows, dripping yellow straws.
There will be plenty of time now, time that will smell of fires,
And drying leather, and catalogues, and apple cores.
  The farmers clean their boots, and whittle, and drowse.

Jeanne McGahey

Legacy

The year has made her will: she left to me
A private purse:
Silver and copper from the dogwood tree,
White gold from a torrent, amber from a pond
And, for my sadness' sake,
Mountains in a bluescape of beyond.
It might be worse:
These will be useful when I lie awake.

                              Christopher Morley

A Patch of Old Snow

There's a patch of old snow in a corner
        That I should have guessed
Was a blow-away paper the rain
        Had brought to rest.

It is speckled with grime as if
        Small print overspread it,
The news of a day I've forgotten—
        If I ever read it.

                              Robert Frost

Reflections on a Gift

of Watermelon Pickle

Received from a Friend

Called Felicity

During that summer
When unicorns were still possible;
When the purpose of knees
Was to be skinned;
When shiny horse chestnuts
(Hollowed out
  Fitted with straws
  Crammed with tobacco
  Stolen from butts
  In family ashtrays)
Were puffed in green lizard silence
While straddling thick branches
Far above and away
From the softening effects
Of civilization;

During that summer—
Which may never have been at all;
But which has become more real
Than the one that was—
Watermelons ruled.

Thick pink imperial slices
Melting frigidly on sun-parched tongues
Dribbling from chins;
Leaving the best part,
The black bullet seeds,
To be spit out in rapid fire
Against the wall
Against the wind
Against each other;

And when the ammunition was spent,
There was always another bite:
It was a summer of limitless bites,
Of hungers quickly felt
And quickly forgotten
With the next careless gorging.

The bites are fewer now.
Each one is savored lingeringly,
Swallowed reluctantly.

But in a jar put up by Felicity,
The summer which maybe never was
Has been captured and preserved.
And when we unscrew the lid
And slice off a piece
And let it linger on our tongue:
Unicorns become possible again.

                    John Tobias